Rain

Written by Meg Stein
Illustrated by Roberto Fino

It rained on Monday.

I went outside.

I got wet.

It rained on Tuesday.

I put on my raincoat.

I went outside.

My feet got wet.

It rained on Wednesday.

I put on my raincoat and my boots.

I went outside.

My head got wet.

It rained on Thursday.

I put on my raincoat,
my boots,
and my hat.

I went outside.

My hands got wet.

It rained on Friday.

I put on my raincoat,
my boots,
my hat,
and my gloves.

I went outside.

My neck got wet.

It rained on Saturday.

I put on my raincoat,
my boots,
my hat,
my gloves,
and my scarf.

I went outside.

The sun came out,
and I got hot.

I took off my raincoat,
my boots,
my hat,
my gloves,
and my scarf.

15

It rained on Sunday.

I didn't go outside.